thriving GIRL DAD

A DUDE'S *Guide* TO RAISING DAUGHTERS

BRIAN YOUNG

Contents

Introduction: It's A Girl...1

Chapter One: Foundation – You 9

Chapter Two: Foundation – Her 23

Chapter Three: Be Intentional – Know Her..........................37

Chapter Four: Self-Worth...49

Chapter Five: Discipline – Setting Boundaries......................59

Chapter Six: Purity 73

Chapter Seven: Endurance...83

"But I'll take the hand of those who don't know the way, who can't see where they are going. I'll be a personal guide to them, directing them through unknown country. I'll be right there showing them what roads to take, make sure they don't fall in the ditch"
Isaiah 42:16

INTRODUCTION
It's a Girl

If you're looking for someone with a long history of counseling families or a long list of letters behind their name that probably makes them a doctor of some sort or an "expert at anything," you've got the wrong guy. I am a dude, just like you. I have climbed the corporate ladder; I have sweat the bills at the end of the month, lost a job, tried to keep in shape, loved my wife well, tried to serve others well, dabbled at a few hobbies and dealt with a whole host of other things while raising four incredible daughters. I have juggled the life that you're juggling.

Over twenty-two years ago, I was handed my first daughter, and I've been blessed with three more angels since that first time. With each one, I became extremely emotional. Not because I was scared or worried (okay maybe a little scared), but because I felt a love like no other. It's one thing to love your wife; however, love for your child is so different. It is even greater with girls. It's instant. It's deep. It's remarkable. While this job will be the hardest you'll ever have, it's also the most rewarding you'll ever have. Now, don't get me wrong. I didn't have a clue what to do. As you'll read later in the book, I often defaulted to my instincts: the instinct of raising my girls like boys.

The day that you are handed your daughter…*Oh snap! What do I do? I'm not ready for this. She isn't a boy!* If you had been handed a boy, no problem. Even though you're a man, let's be honest, at your core, you're still a boy. You probably thought through what you would do with your boy. You would teach him all the things that boys should do. However, here you have been gifted a girl. This fragile angel is now your responsibility. You quickly begin to think, *I don't do girl! I haven't even figured out my wife.* I've got good news for you: your bride does girl, and she can help you.

I thought I had it together when it came to being a dad. I had a great upbringing, parents that modeled what it meant to provide for, care for and protect their little boy. I was raised in the church, so from a young age, I knew right from wrong. My parents loved me dearly and disciplined with love as well. They were involved in my activities and invested in my becoming who I am today. Even with such great examples as a child, it took my lovely bride of twenty-six years to help guide me in raising our girls. To this day, she warns me when I start to parent my girls like they are boys and cheers me on when I get it right. I would not be who I am today, in so many ways, including being a girl dad, without her love. Lean into your wife. Listen and learn from her experience. Yes, I am very fortunate to have wise counsel and a cheerleader in my home.

However, being the girl dad I am today was also made possible with the counsel of many other great people. I have always been open to others' experiences, thoughts and guidance along the way. Other voices have spoken truth to me so I could see past the next hurdle. Very early on, I was asked to be a part of a group of dads who all wanted to be the best dads that they could be. We challenged each other to make the role of dad be extremely important every day! To this day, I have brothers and sisters that spur me on to be better. They inspire me by sharing great stories of the dad–daughter adventure. I promise to share some of these great stories as we travel together.

I invite you on this journey. I promise to share with honesty all that I have done, both wrong and right. For good measure, each of my girls will chime in at the end of each chapter to validate my honesty and the importance of the chapter. Please lean in with honesty as well. Listen to my guidance and put it into practice. Now, I must give caution: Be certain that regardless of your spot on the journey, this will be a battle, a battle within an even larger war. The world wants to raise your little girl. It wants to create her identity. It wants all of her. It especially wants her heart. It wants to do what you were created to do. You need to have a bit of righteous anger against the world that is fighting for your daughter's heart.

God will provide the armor and the cover; however, you must provide the fight. Be the man and dig deep. Take a deep breath. Move your feet to the edge. Let's jump in together. You will feel that rush and great emotion as you dive in. I will be your guide. Through this journey, you will emerge as your daughter's protector. The warrior that every little girl looks for in life. The person that provides for all her needs and then some.

If you don't play the role of the warrior, someone else will get her attention and take your place. If you stick with me, I promise to give you the tools to fight for your daughter's heart!

The YOUNG Girls

Abi, 22

There is nothing better than walking through the front door to a big hug from my dad. As I have gone through twenty-two years of life, my dad's hugs have always been one of my favorite things. The relationship that my dad and I have is deeply rooted in moments in which he has been there to listen to me, encourage me, and counsel me. The connection a daughter has with her dad is incomparable. Even when she is married and creating her own family, she will always want to run to her father (and hopefully, because you have raised her that way, to her Heavenly Father as well).

Though your daughter is like her mother in many obvious ways, she also wants to be just like you! When I picked to go to Baylor University, my dad's alma mater (now mine), my heart grew fond of the new connections we began to share. My last day in Waco, Dad came up to help me move, and we took a long walk around campus, trading memories and reflecting on our time as Baylor students. My dad not only spent quality time with me, he also shared glimpses of his life so I could know him more. It's moments like this one that I will cherish forever.

Dads, do not grow weary because you don't have a little boy to make your mini-me. I can promise you your daughter will want to be right on your heels doing everything you are. I remember a picture of my dad and me (probably age four). As he was building a playset, I stood right beside him with a pencil in my hand.

You will forever and always be her hero! Be steadfast in the effort from the get-go, and when she is older, you'll be able to watch her do amazing things for the glory of the kingdom!

Madi, 21

Hey, Dads, it's Madi. I'm Brian's second oldest daughter. Let me warn you, you're in for a crazy ride, not only throughout this book, but all through life with your daughter(s).

My dad was lucky enough to be blessed with four girls. I don't know where you stand on the daughter count, but no matter the number, your daughter will challenge you in ways unimaginable. We girls have hearts that yearn for true love, care and relationships. We want someone to be there for us and protect us no matter what happens. The *best* person for that job is our dad! Dads are meant to be our heroes, the one who we can run to at all times. Little girls are mistaken when they believe that one day a boy in armor riding on a white horse will come save them. Really that man has been there all along. Fight for her heart! Save her from turning to other things through life because, truly, she wants to be able to turn to you.

Emi, 19

Ever since I was young, I have seen my dad as a role model, someone to go to for encouragement and support. One vivid memory that comes to mind is when I was trying to decide if I should leave basketball, a sport that I knew very well, and begin an unknown sport, softball.

As a sophomore, I was playing on varsity and was looking at quite a successful basketball career. As I contemplated the years I had ahead of me in basketball, the softball coach encouraged me to explore the idea of playing on her team. I had not ever touched a softball with the intent of pursuing the sport. This was not an easy decision. However, my dad never questioned my idea of switching from a guaranteed varsity spot to, possibly, a JV spot on softball. Instead, he encouraged me to make the best decision I could by listing out the pros and cons of both opportunities. And that's exactly what I did.

Listen, Dads, as your daughter grows up, her desires and wishes will evolve. As they change, always be there to support them. Give her your view, the good, bad and ugly, but never shoot down any idea without knowing the true reason behind the new adventure. Start this habit when she is young, and she will always look to you for solid guidance. She will never be fearful to come to you in any situation.

Lili, 18

I have a very unique perspective as the youngest Young daughter. I have experienced how my dad works extremely hard to know each of us and how we're wired. I have watched him love on and parent each of us in a way that is unique to us.

When it comes to me, he has parented a girl my age three times already. He has been there, done that. However, since we are very different from each other, he does not parent us in the same way. He works from his experiences with my older sisters but doesn't presume that I can be parented just like them.

Admittedly, I can get lost in the shuffle being the youngest. Amidst the crazy of being one of four girls, he finds me where I am and makes me feel special. Please allow my dad to guide you through this daughter-raising journey. He knows a thing or two because he's done a thing or two.

"he is like a man building a house, who dug deep and laid the foundation on the rock. And when a flood arose, the stream broke against that house and could not shake it, because it had been well built."
Luke 6:48

CHAPTER ONE
FOUNDATION – YOU

The aroma of diesel fuel was filling up my car. I couldn't see out of my left eye. What just happened? I heard what seemed to be a man's voice screaming, "Get me out!" Oh my goodness, the smell of diesel means something might blow! I have to get out!

Tomorrow is not guaranteed.

August 19, 2014, was a beautiful day. I was headed to a meeting in East Texas. A drive that I had made so many times. I was forty-four years old, a successful business man with a bride of over twenty years that I dearly loved and four beautiful daughters. What else would a guy want? Up to this point, a life well lived.

Then *BOOM!*

What had been a clear view in front of my car became a bright white, and I could not see a thing. Everything shook around me. My world became the screeching of tires and the smell of fumes. Because I had been on this road so many times, I knew where the median was, and I instinctively turned my car towards it to avoid hitting whatever was in front of me. It turned out a semi-tractor trailer had hit a highway striping truck, which caused them to jackknife and suck me into the vortex of the wreck.

In an instant, the beautiful day had taken a significant wrong turn. In a split second, my life sped through my mind just before I hit the side of the striping truck. Inches to the right, and I might have been seriously injured, if not killed. Thank goodness I had veered away from the center of the wreck.

The airbag had forced my sunglasses into my left eye, leaving me temporarily blind. The man's voice had apparently come from the truck that I had just hit. As the strong aroma of diesel fuel continued to fill my car, I released my seatbelt, opened the door and ran towards the back of my car. I was honestly fearful of a fire erupting, or worse, an explosion. I got far back enough from the wreck to see complete destruction: The driver of the semitruck was sitting on the ground complaining about extreme pain, and the other driver had finally escaped the cab of his large truck. The diesel fuel permeated the air even at this distance. Our three vehicles had become mangled metal, and sirens screamed as they began to approach.

All of this seemed to happen in mere seconds, yet time also passed by in slow motion. It was surreal as I tried to make sense of it all.

The paramedics checked me out, and thank goodness, all seemed to be fine. Unfortunately, the other drivers were not as lucky. Both appeared to be injured and were taken to the hospital. My bride and a good friend arrived pretty quickly after I was cleared to go. It was so comforting to see familiar faces, as I slipped into Dee's car, I was overcome with emotion. *What if?* rushed through mind. *What if* my car had been just feet to the right as I hit the truck? *What if* I was seriously hurt or, worse, killed? This question of "what if?" consumed my thoughts. One of the most significant what-ifs was, "Have I done the right things in raising my girls?"

Had I done enough in their short lives to carry them the rest of their lives? I had been a good dad. But had I been fully fighting on their behalf? Fighting while they were young so that when they entered the teen years and beyond, I'd be the one they would go to for answers to life's questions? Would I be in their world, or would I be shut out because others and things of this world had captured their hearts?

Soon after that wreck, God gave me a gift. A gift that would help me answer that haunting question, "Have I done the right things in raising my girls?" My gift was being chosen as the speaker at our church's Brave conference, a conference for dads and their daughters to learn more about each other and grow closer.

What does it mean to be brave? Webster's defines brave as "ready to face and endure danger or pain; showing courage." Am I brave? What a question to ask after being invited to a "Brave" conference. But I believed that I had been as a dad, though I found that I became much braver with God's help. In preparation for my talk, I slowed down the parts of my life that rushed through my mind the day of the wreck. I recalled being handed each of my precious daughters when they were born. I was so scared. *How could I be responsible for a girl?* I'm sure you can relate to that feeling. Memories flooded back to me of the early years, where I mostly got it wrong. Raising my voice, being selfish with my time, crushing their hearts and making them cry. The memories of when I matured as a father were much better. Loving on them, listening to them (not solving their problems), reading the Bible together and one of them calling shotgun every time I was about to leave the house to run errands. I stood on that stage and poured out my heart about doing it right and allowed them to see what doing it wrong looks like through my mistakes. It was real because our calling as dads is real. I walked off that stage absolutely spent and honored to share my experiences.

Raising a daughter, never mind four, is a daunting task. At times it can seem nearly impossible. The good news is that it is so very possible, and you can thrive as a dad. The one thing that has been clear throughout my journey is that I can't do this alone. I've mentioned my bride, Dee, and all the others that have walked this road with me; however, only one has truly made any of it possible.

I have found time and time again that my Savior, Jesus Christ, is the most powerful force, counselor and friend for this adventure. Now, you might not have an understanding of the Lord or the power He possesses, and that's okay. You might not know Him; however, my prayer is that you would discover Him and learn how He is the most important asset for this important task. He possesses the tools for this fight.

As a young man, I accepted Christ on the front porch of my childhood home. I knew who He was by going to church growing up, but on the afternoon of my salvation, I was desperate for help. I won't go into detail, but my best friend, who had moved away, found himself in trouble. I had heard that He could and would help those that followed Him in all situations.

I was in a situation, and I needed help.

I cried out to Him and said the prayer. "Lord, I believe you walked this earth as a perfect man, died on a cross for my sins and rose from the dead. I want you to be the Lord of my life…" Boom, I was saved. It seemed so simple; however, I did not grasp the responsibility of the prayer I had prayed. I accepted the salvation, but I honestly did not know what it was truly like to "walk with the Lord."

Many years later, I was in my late twenties with two daughters and plans for more. I had not acted out my faith as a young man, never mind a father. It hit me like a ton of bricks, much like it did you, that I needed to be the example in so many ways to my daughters. First and foremost, I had to raise the bar on being a man of faith and live it out in front of my girls. Now all eyes were on me.

After many visits to our new church in Rockwall, Dee and I decided to become members. One of the first questions asked of us was, "Have you both been baptized?" Of course my lovely bride boldly stated that she had been properly baptized. However, I had not. Let's define "properly baptized." I had been sprinkled with holy water in the church as a teen as a sign of my acceptance of Christ. Dee, and the church we were joining, believed that proper baptism was attained through immersion. Immersion is how John the Baptist baptized Jesus in the Jordan. This baptism represents Jesus's death, resurrection and our new life in Him.

At first I took offense to this notion; however, after studying the scripture, I agreed with my wife. While I agreed with her, though, the catalyst for my baptism/rededication of my faith in

Jesus was my daughters. With a new town, a new church and a family that I was responsible for, I wanted a new faith. A faith that was outward, one that my daughters would see as an example of Jesus. I was and still am that guy that doesn't always set the best example; however, I strive daily to.

But, Brian, you don't know my backstory. You don't know the family I grew up in. How can I do what I don't know? Or maybe you're saying, *Dude, I got this. Not a problem.* I grew up in a Christian home. I read my Bible and attend church regularly.

I don't know which of these men you are; however, we can't continue this journey together without you answering the question: "How solid is *my* foundation?"

Is it solid enough to support your girls, who desperately need an example of Christ? Regardless of how you answered this question, know that God provides grace and power. Grace that surpasses wherever you are in Christ and power to thrive as a dad. Please, hear me. You have to get yourself in training daily so you are what your daughter needs. You can't build her foundation unless you have one.

Trust me when I say, this is the most important part of being a dad. Your daughters will struggle in walking with the Heavenly Father if you aren't walking with your Heavenly Father.

Now, this might get a little uncomfortable. You are a guy, so you can take it. Ask yourself a few questions to do an honest evaluation of your foundation:

- Do I truly have a personal relationship with Jesus?
- Do I spend time in the Word?
- Do I attend a local church?

- Do I pray daily/constantly?
- Do I associate with the "right" crowd?
- Do I have fellowship with other believers?
- Do I act out my faith?
- Do I have someone holding me accountable?

Okay, maybe I didn't give you enough warning. That might have been more than uncomfortable. *Brian, that flat-out hurt.* I know, these hurt me too. I was asked these questions as a young dad because I needed it, and so do you. "Put on the full armor of God, so that you can take your stand against the devil's schemes" (Ephesians 6:11). We need hard questions so we can have our full armor ready for battle. Now that I have sucker-punched you, please remember this: grace is available in the process.

Though you hopefully already answered the questions above, let's really look at them, together. Regardless of where you are on your personal journey, I have to begin with the most important question: "Do you truly have a personal relationship with Jesus?" This singular idea is the core of your foundation.

If you have never made the decision to have this relationship, please pray and make that happen. As much as we are taught as men to do it all on our own, we need someone braver than us to lead the way. You need an example to follow. If you are not ready for this decision, don't stop reading. Instead, do me a favor: simply ask God if He is real. The Bible says to draw near to God so that He may draw near to you.

You must begin your day connected to Heaven. Christ wants to be a part of your adventure every day, especially in the raising of your daughter. I worked hard for many years to make time with the Lord a daily routine. Think of it as connecting with your best friend, coach, boss, leader, etc., for guidance and a glimpse at the game plan. Prayer is the best way to connect. Just have a man-to-man conversation. Ask for guidance for your steps as a father. Ask God how to lead your daughter. Listen intently, and take His advice. I promise that you'll need His advice. There are things you will not understand that He can sort out. This is a constant conversation of praise and advice, back and forth daily.

Be in God's Word. Read the ultimate field manual to life. The Bible can be intimidating; however, what I have found is, as I read it, I'm directed to where I need to be. Not every scripture points to "how to raise your daughter," but each gives insight into living life. I'm amazed at how the more I read and study God's Word, the more clarity I have about life.

The words will jump off the page. A situation that you can't figure out will become clear. Allow these words to speak to you. Even if they don't seem to give you the exact answer, comfort and peace will be provided in the midst of your struggles and questions. If you live life according to scripture, your daughter will see it in you. *You* have to know God's Word before you have a shot at teaching it to your daughter.

Just as you need His power and advice, so does your daughter. The Bible will answer the questions you have on the journey and offer the answers to her questions as well.

How long has it been since you attended church? I hope, for most of you, it is habit. Not a required attendance, but a connection to God in fellowship.

All of us want others in the trenches battling for the same ideals. Church is an opportunity to lay the cards on the table and admit we need help in the battle. You will find out that other men want what you want. You want to do it right and grow as a father. If you do attend church, find a small group of folks to share life with.

The smaller the group, the deeper you will go. Be honest with each other and grow together. This isn't a place for prideful conversation. It's a place for honesty. The ultimate would be a small group of men with which to really go deep, an accountability group that shares and holds tightly your deepest desires and struggles. Fellowship is required and much needed for this journey.

Are you serving others? The culmination of your faith is acting upon it. We can't just accept Him, read about Him, pray to Him and have fellowship, without action. Men are called to act, so why not act in your faith? We were designed to make things happen. We do it in our jobs, in sports and in a host of other things, so why not take action on what we believe? As the old saying goes, "Actions speak louder than words!" Serving is the result of all the other things you do in faith. You build your faith through action, like a muscle that needs flexing, if you will.

Early on in my faith journey as a dad, I was asked to go on a mission trip to Russia. I know, just the idea scared the stuff out of me. Excuses poured into my mind and out of my mouth. I didn't know the Bible, I hadn't ever shared my faith and never mind the fact that Russia is halfway around the world.

After all the excuses and reasons why not, I went on that first trip, and on many more after that one. That first step of service led me to adventures, countries, relationships and experiences that would have never been a part of my story without my trusting the Lord. Serving has built who I am today. Most importantly, my girls watched me go serve, and it led to us serving together. Serving with your daughter will create the richest memories of your time with her. I promise! Is your faith evident in your life? You have to mimic Jesus with your life. Your daughter is watching you. You may say a lot to her; however, what you do will make the greatest impact.

Do the people you associate with point you towards Jesus or away? Take an inventory of your friends. Are they the people that you would let your daughter hang with? How's your mouth? Do you use "big boy" words that are not appropriate? I understand the struggle. Living in a "man's" world isn't easy. The lure of acting badly is real. Christ was the best example of a man, so why not emulate Him and not the world? If you act like Him, your daughter will look for Him!

Okay, the foundation has been explained. You *can* move forward without His power—but oh how much harder it will be. The struggle is going to be present, so why not tap in the maker of the universe to help you in the fight?

I know most people have a vision of Christ as being meek and mild. Yes, He was and so should you be, at times; however, you can connect to the "warrior" side of Jesus. The brave leader. Exodus describes Jesus in this way: "The Lord is a warrior, the Lord is His name." Can you conjure up an image of Mel Gibson in *Braveheart*? He pleads with his countrymen to "fight." They had a common cause of freedom, and William Wallace led the way. He was the hero of the story. You get a chance to fight for your daughter and be the hero.

Hear me, you are not going to bat a thousand. Think *work in progress*. Cracks will appear. Be humble daily as to where you need to shore up your foundation. I guarantee you that a cracked foundation that is being improved daily is better than no foundation at all.

The YOUNG Girls

Abi, 22

There cannot be enough emphasis on this. The spiritual foundation you set is *key* to the upbringing of your daughters. Set an example with your words and actions. Be sure your girls see you diving into the Word daily and hear you referencing scriptures. They will tune in to these things as they grow in their faith.

As I created a life for myself away from home, I also built my own independent faith. If it was not for the spiritual guidance of my father (and mother), my path would have been a little bit different. I know that if I ever have any questions or doubts, I can go to my dad, assured he will come from a scriptural standpoint.

Madi, 21

Having a strong-believing dad will provide your daughter with a little less of a bumpy road as she discovers her own faith. She can come to you with questions and be able to find answers there instead of trying to find them somewhere else. In her society today, who knows where she would otherwise look to find those answers. I ask that you take the action steps throughout the book seriously.

Don't move forward in this book until you have begun your foundation with Jesus. Your daughter will appreciate it. :) I know I appreciated my dad being solid in his faith. I remember from a very young age always having a place for Jesus in our home. He was truly a part of our everyday lives. Thanks to my strong faith-centered upbringing I am now able to have a personal relationship with Jesus.

Emi, 19

How do you want your daughter to turn out? What do you want her life to look like while she is in your home? What example is she going to see? The world's, or the example you set through your faith? What she is exposed to is what she will mimic. Unfortunately, the life of girls is heavily influenced by alcohol, drugs, vaping, sex, etc. In a girl's eyes, these things allow her to have the guy she wishes for or enables her to reach her dreams. If you allow the model of Christian faith to be her example through you, she will have a better chance of avoiding these worldly desires. You are showing what a Godly man and Godly life look like so she knows that she doesn't have to act like the stereotypical girl.

Lili, 18

For as long as I can remember we have been in church as a family. My dad has made it a priority. We have attended church on the weekends and the many events available for us to be involved in. My dad has taught me and my friends from a young age and he still does even now that I'm a teenager. He encourages us to do the right things in life. I'm able to go to him for answers to difficult questions and receive guidance.

TAKE ACTION

- Find a local church to attend weekly.

- Become a member of a Sunday school class/life group.

- Create an accountability group with like-minded men.

- Create time daily to read your Bible.

- Make prayer a habit.

- Create friend groups to reflect Christ.

- Serve in some capacity.

According to the grace of God given to me,
like a skilled master builder I laid a foundation,
and someone else is building upon it. Let each
one take care how he builds upon it."
1 Corinthians 3:10

CHAPTER TWO
FOUNDATION – HER

When I was a kid, our family would spend a lot of summers on a lake that spanned both Texas and Oklahoma. It was touted, by my dad, as the largest man-made lake in either state. You could ride in a boat for what seemed like hours and never touch land. It was one of my favorite places. A place to be with my family and just have fun.

One of the biggest attractions on the lake was the collection of large sand islands in the middle of it. We'd pull our boat right up on the sand, throw out the anchor and spend the day. You felt like you were on some deserted island, able to explore and possibly find hidden treasure. Of course, as you can imagine with all that sand, what else would you do besides build sand castles? I would spread out all of my buckets, shovels, shells and whatever else fueled my imagination. I would do my very best to fortify my castle; however, it never failed that either the tide or my poorly built walls would cave it in.

After a lot of trial and error mixed with a lot of frustration, my dad would come to the rescue. My dad was a custom-home builder. He had spent many years designing, planning and building houses. He would always stress the importance of a solid foundation. Since he could build strong foundations for houses, he was surely knowledgeable enough to build a strong sand castle. We'd flatten out a well-packed sand foundation, and away we would go. We'd build until it was perfect. Nothing elaborate, just solid. Solid enough to withstand the "storms of the beach." Over and over, he'd share the knowledge that he had about foundations and home-building. A knowledge that was created over years of experience.

Now that you've survived your foundation-building challenge, let's turn towards the harder task—your daughter's foundation. No worries. You have an understanding of what a solid foundation looks like, and now you just need to help her achieve the same.

As you already learned, I did not have it all together when I began having girls. I was challenged in so many ways. Be humble with your daughter. You will not have all the answers, and there is no shame in her knowing that.

But your growth, just like mine was, will be parallel to the growth of your daughter. Think of it like this: You will have to train then coach, train then coach. Sometimes you'll train in private, and sometimes you'll train so your daughter can observe your training.

Your daughter must understand that her identity is in Christ. Christ alone! I like to say that she is "performing for an audience of ONE!" Christ being the ONE. You have to introduce her to Him and understand that she might not understand at first; however, with a daily introduction, she will get it. She has to know that a decision for Him is the most important decision that she will ever make. I began with simple childhood Bibles and built upon the stories as my girls grew older. As they understood more, I introduced more. The idea of having a relationship with Jesus, someone your daughter cannot see, can be confusing, so go at her pace. The great part is that she will guide you with questions as she understands. Be prepared. As she understands more, you might get a question for which you don't know the answer. This is an opportunity for you to go seek the answer alone or to go searching together. Either way is appropriate. Let me be clear, your most important task in this foundation-building is introducing her to Jesus and having her accept Him as her own. Don't panic if it takes years for her to make that decision. You just keep making the introduction, and God will do His thing.

Use the following tools to help you:

Bible. The cornerstone of this foundation. Even before your daughter can talk, she needs to hear the words of the Bible. She must know the stories in the Bible, which shows the character of God and contains all the answers to every question she will ever have.

As I mentioned above, I started with Bible picture books with simple stories. When it was just Abi, I would sit her in my lap and thumb through the pages of these picture books. As our family grew, doing this became part of our family time together before bed. We built a routine of bath and Bible time. Don't make it complicated, and don't get frustrated as I did when they don't always pay attention. I promise they hear every word. As they grow up, grab the Bible and study it together. This holy habit will lead them to incredible discoveries about their creator, to the stories of faith and most importantly to a personal relationship with Christ.

Prayer. What a powerful connection to God. I began early, making sure my girls knew how to speak with and listen to God through prayer. We began by praying over them when they were babies. They needed to hear me speak with the Lord. It was very important that they knew how to speak to Him and that they knew their dad was dependent on Him as well.

As they began to speak as little girls, we taught them how to pray. When they're young, it is so simple and sweet. Let them repeat after you so they understand what prayer sounds like. Express your love, thank God for your blessings, and ask Him for care and guidance. Kneel beside their bed; lie down beside them if there is room.

Just as it is with a close friend, we can't know them if we don't spend time with them in conversation. Your daughter needs a friend that is always there to listen, help, comfort and guide her. Even more important than you, God has to be who she leans into. She needs to know that God is always present and that she can talk with Him at any time.

Dee and I have a tradition of praying with our daughters that has lasted over twenty years. We pray with our girls every night before bed. It began as something that we pushed and made sure happened. Even as they have gotten older, as they head to bed, they ask, "Are you coming to pray?" If I'm not able to be with them by their beds, I make it happen on the phone. I have stepped away from the dinner table while conducting business, taken breaks during meetings—whatever it takes to pray with my girls. This tradition is so well known by friends and business colleagues, that they remind me, or if others notice I'm missing, someone quickly says, "Brian's praying with his girls." I promise this time of prayer will grow a bond with your daughters like no other.

I vividly remember sitting in a booth at an important work dinner in Atlanta, Georgia. It was getting late, and I knew prayer time was quickly approaching. There was a catch. I was at the table with important folks who I didn't want to disappoint by leaving the table, not to mention, I was in the corner of the booth, so it would be very disruptive if I left. No just slipping away to the "restroom." I had to make a decision: stay and avoid possible repercussions or hold fast to the prayer-time tradition. I took that risk and got out of the booth. I walked away from the table with a sense of pride since I knew it was the right decision; however, worry lingered.

I prayed with my girls, and when I returned to the table, the men asked, "How was your call?" I explained what the tradition was, and to my surprise, they were impressed by the importance I put on this time with my girls. That experience gave me a boldness to always carry on the tradition, regardless of circumstance. Set the bar for yourself, for your daughter, and you may be surprised by whom you'll influence along the way.

Community. I was reminded recently that you become who you associate with, so exposing your angel to a church community is so important. She needs to experience fellowship, worship, God's Word and friendship. Thriving in life requires like-minded people that one can count on for the journey. Though I grew up in the church, I didn't fully grasp the importance and beauty of being a part of a church community until later in life. In college,

I even took a "break" from going to church. I believed that God knew me, and I knew Him, and that that's all that mattered. Not so. I was abruptly reminded of the importance of going to church on my first date with my bride.

As our date ended on a Saturday night, Dee asked, "Where do you attend church?" I made a solid mistake by hesitating and spouting where I went to church growing up. Wrong answer. Dee looked me straight in the eyes and said, "If you're going to date me, we'll be in church every weekend." Loud and clear. And guess what? We have not missed church many times since that first date. Also, because of that humbling moment, I have enjoyed a community like no other.

You will need the help of others in raising your daughter. Begin with the normal dropping her off in the children's area while you attend church. She will learn Bible lessons and begin forming a group of friends. At an early age, she starts to understand the importance of good friends. As she gets older, involve her in a Sunday school class. Here, she really begins to learn more about following Jesus and true friendship.

Please know that friendship is huge for a girl. Much more than it is for us. So this church community becomes more important as she grows older.

As the school years begin, your daughter will continue forming community. Now, this community could include some of the same friends; however, most will not be there. Regardless, just as we should "huddle up" at church to take on the world, so should your daughter. She has to have a safe harbor of friends that accept her for who she is and hold her accountable to who she wants to become in Christ. For this reason, involving your daughter in a youth group as she enters middle school is so important. At youth school, children have great adults beside them and form friends that will carry them through high school. At this juncture, kids begin to choose their paths, which impacts their lives in such a massive way. Don't be afraid to get involved in this community with them. The years of being in a youth group are so much fun but also critical for the future.

Dee and I have raised our girls in community. When my girls were young, we would have friends from our church group over to the house. Some of these families' kids are the same ones that our girls would hang out with throughout school. Kids would run throughout the house and backyard. We as young parents would "huddle up" to discuss life. What we didn't realize was that we were setting an example of community for our kids. They're watching.

Service. I really didn't understand what it meant to serve until a dear friend challenged me to go on my first mission trip. He didn't ask me to simply go downtown and feed the homeless. As mentioned before, I was invited on an adventure to Communist Russia. I was absolutely scared to death. I felt unqualified, unworthy and, honestly, clueless about what I was being asked to do. But I now know that invitation was truly an invitation from God to be a part of His work. I had to understand that God doesn't call the equipped; He equips the called. I was called and He equipped me. What I did not realize was, when I left on this trip and many others since then, my girls were watching. They were watching me serve. They saw me acting out my faith.

We have made serving a big part of our family. Just this last summer, we were all on mission around the world. My wife and I took our senior in high school to South Africa along with a handful of members from our youth group. The crazy thing is that we met up with our sophomore in college, who was staying in the same area for an entire month.

The three of us were able to love on both adults and kids suffering from HIV AIDS, teach life skills and serve alongside youth groups in the local villages. While we were halfway around the world, our junior in high school was on staff at a youth camp we helped start years prior. She got to be a lifeguard and love on kids. While this was all happening, our oldest served at a large youth camp near Houston. She spent her second summer serving at camp. What an incredible summer that was, built on a tradition of serving. A tradition that didn't "just happen" but that's been made a priority as the girls have grown up.

Actions speak louder than words, and faith is an act of obedience. Your daughter needs to act and be obedient. Service is the way to do that. There are always projects to be done around your community. Begin by taking her along as you serve food at a homeless shelter, pass out blankets at a nursing home or stock the local food pantry. She'll get to experience the impact that she can have on another person with simple acts of kindness. She might be a little outside her comfort zone; however, that is not a bad thing. This will prepare her for and help her understand the idea of being a vessel that God uses for His service. When daughters are a vessel, God can use them in ways they couldn't imagine.

As age and experience converge, it will be time for them to

serve on their own. They then decide what they feel is best for them. They will discover their gifts and the talents that God will use in them. Don't be scared when they want to go on a mission trip with their youth group. It is important that they serve at an increasing dependence on God. Their faith will grow and so will yours.

This foundation that you help your daughter build will need reinforcements at times. Each part of it will be challenged by the other things that become priorities in life. As she grows, the world will get her attention, and new issues will arise. But all of these foundational elements will help defend against that. Listen to her and help her build her foundation as things change. Fight to make these activities a priority in her life. I promise she will thank you for it.

The YOUNG Girls

Abi, 22

The spirituality of your daughter (and son if you have one) can arguably be the most important mission you have on earth. We are called to minister to the lost and help bring sight to the blind. This means in your own household. Your children are blind to the grace and mercy the Lord has to offer them until someone introduces them to it, so why not make that person you? There are so many paths you can prevent your daughter from going down if you start following the steps laid out in this chapter. My life would 110% be in a way different direction if it was not for the spiritual leadership that my parents took over us at such a young age. It's special to be bonded not only with your Heavenly Father through faith and relationship, but also with your earthly father through the spirit of Jesus!

The dedication it takes for a father to introduce his daughter to Jesus and be that example for her is the biggest gift you can give her. It will be difficult to keep her on the straight and narrow, but I *promise* when she is mature enough to understand, she will eternally be grateful for the foundation you set before her.

The second I left home for college and was introduced to the "real" world, I realized all the ways that my parents guarded my heart and set me up for a life full of value. It's hard when you're in middle school and high school and everyone around you is setting their eyes on the world around them. It was my church community, which my parents helped foster, that encouraged me to not stray from what Jesus called me to. Because of the decision my parents made long before I was born, to raise us in a Christ-centered home that served the Lord, I am able to stand confidently in faith, knowing full well who my Savior is.

Madi, 21

One of the biggest problems I saw growing up regarding fathers was that they put up one of two faith fronts: "I know everything" or "I know nothing." *I know everything*—this is when a father fails to be relatable, open or vulnerable with their children (especially daughters), preventing trust in their relationship. Your daughter will begin to feel you are too perfect for her and turn to someone who is more relatable for that trust and connection. *I know nothing*—when parents disconnect from faith altogether, they push their children in one way or another. Your daughter will have to go on this journey alone, again resorting to finding others she can trust, or she will decide to turn from faith as well. When you go to either extreme, you lose your chance and dismiss your role of fighting for her.

That consequence is not worth it. Be the man your daughter needs in faith so that you both can grow together towards the Lord and an eternity together. My dad has been a figure in my church for as long as I can remember. While I was in middle and high school, my dad was my small group leader at church. He literally took the position as a spiritual leader in my life so that I would grow as well.

Emi, 19

If it was not for watching my dad show God's image, I would probably not have this sound foundation of faith that I do today. There is not a big enough group of girls—or people—around me to show me the same love and support that I have received from my dad because of his unending love and faith through Christ. Because of my faith, I can now identify those things that I need to avoid. My dad's faith gave me the eyes to see what he sees in Jesus, the ultimate example of right and wrong.

Lili, 18

I was always seeing my dad at church, and being with him showed me an example of how we are supposed to serve the Lord and show others Jesus. I love serving because I have been shown what I can do and how I can impact other people.

TAKE ACTION

- Find a good Bible that is age appropriate to read to or with your daughter.

- Make it a daily habit to pray—you'll need an idea of what to pray for and planned times to make it happen.

- Attend a church that serves the purpose of your daughter now and as she grows—one that's child/youth centric.

- Attend events that are focused on your daughter.

- Volunteer at church to be around your daughter's friends.

- Create discussions around Bible lessons, for spiritual growth.

Search me, O God, and know my heart! Try me and know my thoughts!
Psalm 139:23

CHAPTER THREE
BE INTENTIONAL – KNOW HER

I was working my first job out of college. After four years at a private university and a mass of debt, I was given a not-so-well-paying job. I landed the job of "housekeeping manager" or better yet "environmental services manager" at Children's Medical Center of Dallas. Don't get me wrong, it wasn't the job or the title that I wasn't grateful for. I wanted a job in sales. Chart my own course making the big bucks. I really questioned, "What's my purpose?" Let's just say that one of my purposes was completely unexpected.

I was up on 6 East and a quite-attractive young nurse asked for "Ryan?" I politely corrected her on my name and took the phone call that had come to the floor. I wasn't looking for a girlfriend; however, in that moment, I realized I wanted to get to know Dee Parrish.

From that moment until this day, I have worked with all my might to get to know her heart.

You know the story. I did all that I could to cross her path every day. I spent more time "checking" on my team on 6E than on any other floor. If she was moved to another floor, that became the most looked-after part of the hospital. I wanted to know all about this incredible nurse from Tennessee. As I got to know her, I wanted to know her more. Details were key. Topics that I was unfamiliar with became more interesting because I wanted to know her. Any day I spent time with Dee was a great day!

I'm confident that you have a similar story as to how you met the mother of your daughter. You saw something. You saw the fireworks explode every time. You wanted to know everything about her. You wanted to spend every waking hour asking questions. Gathering pieces to the puzzle that you so desperately wanted to be put together. I have to be honest: You will never find all the pieces to the puzzle so it will never be complete. Isn't that so exciting, though? It should be. New incredible discoveries every day. The journey you took and are still taking in getting to know your bride is and should always be top priority; however, now you have a new adventure.

Take that experience of getting to know your wife and apply it to your daughter. Just like your wife, she needs someone, you, to know her. She needs to be pursued with curiosity. From the first time she cries as a baby, you need to know, *Why?*

She needs to know that you care and want to spend time with her regardless of the circumstance. Just as with your wife, if you don't know her, you can't speak to her heart. You can't mold what you don't know. Let's be honest, as with getting to know your spouse, it is not familiar territory: Little girls are quite different than little boys. They want you to ask questions and, more importantly, listen to the answer. Even when you don't understand the situation, listen. Note to self—to know them you have to spend time with them. I know what you're thinking, *Thanks, Captain Obvious.*

Now, I hear you asking, *But how?*

How can I do this with my already-busy life? I have so many things that I have to do or, more importantly, like to do. I have an extremely important career. My job requires long hours. I travel all week long. I have to get that next promotion. Oh, and never mind my hobbies. I love to play golf. I can't skip a workout at the gym. After all of these things, I'm out of time and out of energy.

Yes, you have to provide for your family. Yes, you need to have things that energize you. However, as with all things that are important, you have to create time. You have to create time for your daughter. The work will always ask more of you. The hobbies can be scaled back. Wake up earlier, before she wakes up; stay up after she goes to bed; go to the gym fewer times a week. Don't lose who you are or neglect your responsibilities— just be better at scheduling your life to include more of her. I speak from experience: the time to spend time with your angel is fleeting, so take advantage of every moment. Hang tight, and I will give you a little secret to doing this in a minute.

To be honest, getting to know my daughters wasn't and isn't always easy. Girls do girl stuff. It starts at a young age with baby dolls, dress-up, tea parties, princess movies…As they grow up, it becomes shopping, getting their nails done, girl drama…You're in unfamiliar territory that you must become a part of. Your love for your daughter has to supersede what you like or dislike. You have to dive into her world every day. When she is young, watch how she plays and play with her. As you play, ask a lot of questions. *What are the names of your dolls? What's your favorite part of playing on the swing set?* Be daring and let her do your hair or paint your nails. As she grows older, attend her recitals, coach her sports and participate in school activities. Now, I have to come clean. As I tell anyone that asks, I am grateful that all four of my girls are athletes, so it made time with them much easier as they got older. Now I did have to sit through a few recitals, watch some cheering at football games. With each one of my girls, regardless of knowledge or "interest," I become both knowledgeable and interested.

Spending time with your angel gives her value. Value that the Heavenly Father puts on her and value that you validate with your time and interest in her. The act of affirming her value in this world is paramount. I found that asking questions about her likes and dislikes also helps her define who she is. We will dive deep into this idea later on; however, getting to know her builds on the idea of self-worth. These key questions lead to her understanding her gifts and talents. Once you know these "areas of interest" or her "sweet spots," you begin to understand who she is, and she does the same. We all want to know who we are. You have the privilege of discovering with her. What a treat it has been for me. I promise it will be for you.

Okay, here's the little secret that I promised earlier. How can you make this process so much easier? Wait for it. Ask yourself, *What am I good at? What do I enjoy?* Include your daughter in *your* "sweet spot." Most of your hobbies and work are built around your gifts and talents. Look at what work and hobbies you can involve her in. Can she go to work with you and learn about what you do for a living? Or simply share with her on a regular basis what's going on at work. I have always been in the medical field, so my girls have been intrigued by what I do. We often talk about my day. What issues I'm having at work, what technology I'm selling or where my trip for work has taken me.

Let them come along when you go to the driving range, let them work out with you, or simply let them be a part of a project around the house. I made it a tradition to never run an errand without one of my girls with me. Always, a Young daughter was riding shotgun or, when they were younger, sitting in the back seat as I did my things.

Here's what's crazy: they might just make your hobby their hobby as they get older. I spent many years competing in triathlons. My girls would watch me train. At times, I would sit on my bike trainer in the living room so I could still be with my girls. They would attend my races, and in time, I got to watch them compete in triathlons.

Make time to include them in your interests, and you will get to know them in the process. As shared in my story, I began to see my gifts, talents and interests align with my daughter's and vice versa. We did things together that we both loved and in that built an incredible relationship.

As the years roll along, your daughter will scream for a cell phone so she can connect to the world. Stand firm on delaying this launch as long as you can. Dee and I held the line until our girls were in middle school, knowing they would need to connect with us for pick-up times and things like that. We held firm because we knew a phone would open up a Pandora's box to the world and what comes with it. We set boundaries, which I will discuss in a later chapter.

However, I found a new way to connect with my girls with this tool. This one addition allowed me to touch them from a far. Now, please listen, this does not replace face-to-face connectivity. This is an addition to your daily habits of connecting. I can text them a simple "I love you" or a scripture for the day, or have a quick chat. I can be anywhere and feel like we are in the same room. If you are super cool, try FaceTiming. What an amazing way to see her precious face and keep up with each other.

To get to know her, how about diving into the social media sites that she follows? The things she follows will tell you a lot about her. You have the ability to see her world from her perspective. So much is said by what she follows and shows interest in. You also get to see her posts and enjoy her life when she is not with you. By understanding her social media life, you can create topics and activities for the time you do spend together.

Please don't miss this opportunity. Knowing your daughter and her heart sets you up to succeed in so many areas. Her heart will tell you everything. Knowing her heart provides you the gift of listening to it, protecting it and sensing what it needs as she grows. It sounds so basic, but it is a critical factor in being the dad that God designed you to be.

You knowing and being known by your daughter builds trust. Trust is so fundamental. Do you listen to people you don't trust? Of course not. Build that trust through time together. Now, go spend time with your daughter.

The YOUNG Girls

Abi, 22

Quality time is my love language. I did not really understand what that meant nor how I enjoy interacting with people until I was in college. Now that I know that about myself, it makes complete sense why my childhood memories are some of my favorite and why my family is who I like being around the most. It's because we spent great quality time together. My mom and dad did a wonderful job at keeping us connected when we were young. Even though sometimes we whined about going to the store all together or watching Madi's basketball games when we wanted to stay at home, those moments of being all together can never be replaced.

Specifically with my dad, two things come to mind. Working in medical sales, Dad was always in the OR while doctors used his devices, so with that came many stories. I used to be extremely intrigued by the human cadaveric nerves he used to sell. I would stay up in bed waiting for him to get home so I could hear the cases he was dealing with. I have an extremely weak stomach, so this interest in the medical field didn't take me down a career path in hospitals, *but* it has led me to design them! I now get to have great conversations with my dad about his time in the hospitals so that I can learn how to improve the experience people are having within them. It has really helped my knowledge and skill to be able to do my job better.

The second thing that comes to mind is the time my dad would spend watching and cheering for me as I played volleyball for six years. It warmed my heart to see him on the stands at club practice, tournaments and high school games. He not only connected with me by asking me questions but also built relationships with my teammates and their parents. He, my mom, and I built a community for ourselves through my club teams and high school team. Those memories of sitting for hours waiting on a game, or driving late at night to practice, are filled with great conversation and quality time, which, again, is irreplaceable. Like my dad said, getting to know your daughter is not just about becoming part of her world, but also about bringing her into yours. It's a symbiotic relationship, but I'll be honest with you: I think a lot of my interests are sparked from his.

Recently I have grown a love for running, which is definitely something I got from my dad. Now we enjoy talking at length, exchanging our experiences and joys about the sport. You may just be surprised at what all your daughter takes up that is reflective of you!

Madi, 21

One of the coolest parts of growing up was being part of what my mom and dad loved to do. Whether that was hearing about their Bible study, listening to work stories, being around while they trained/worked out, or even getting out and doing something with them. A few memories that I hold dear to my heart are the trips we took to see my dad race in triathlons (especially his IronMans in Arizona). That was a time I really got to see my dad come alive! He loved using his athletic ability to serve the Lord and create community. We would thrive on our early-morning wake-ups and long days of cheering our dad on! Little did we know soon we would be doing it ourselves because we developed a love for it just like he did.

I love going back and looking at all the pictures taken the day the Young girls embarked on their little triathlon in Rockwall, Texas! I am thankful for the intentional time my dad spent with each of us. It has created a relationship where we feel known and loved by him, which shows us just how much more we are known and loved by our Savior.

Emi, 19

Do you know your daughter? If your answer is *no*, you probably have a major issue. Your daughter does not know you! From experience, some of the most venerable conversation I had with my dad started out with a conversation about what he had on his heart or what he did that day/week. One of the main examples of me getting to know my dad was when he was in love with mountain biking, and I was terrified to ride a bike anywhere close to a mountain. When I was fifteen, my dad had his first mountain-biking experience, at Winter Park, Colorado, and one of the first people he went to tell about it was me, because he believed I would fall in love. This is a prime example of, one, my dad knowing me more than I knew myself by encouraging me to do something I was scared of and, two, something that led to countless one-on-one experiences that created a closer relationship with my dad. Because I knew my dad and trusted his opinion, I was able to step out on a limb and try something new, which now I *have* fallen in love with, and between you and me, I am now better at than him. LOL.

I hope that one day y'all have such a strong trust with your daughter that she'll be willing to step out on a limb and jump into something knew. *But* the only way you can gain her trust is by allowing her to know who you really are and not holding back on things you are not sure she's interested in.

Lili, 18

I started to show interest in my dad's triathlons, specifically swimming. So at a young age, I joined the swim team, and my dad would always encourage me to do well and coach me if he could. I loved how he showed interest in my passions. As I grew up, the rigors of the swim team became too much, so I would go swim with my dad, and that grew our connectivity even more.

Throughout my life I always noticed how my dad would become interested and educated in what I was doing. No matter what it was or whether he was interested or not, he became interested for the sake of getting to know me. One big thing is to always affirm her interests and not think that they're weird or different. That's just your perspective. One thing I liked to do when I was growing up was play Minecraft, which seemed to be more of a boys' game, but my dad, knowing this, still showed interest and thought that my builds were so cool. Looking back, I never felt like what I liked to do was wrong because my dad was always there to encourage me.

TAKE ACTION

- Interview your daughter—pre-write some questions and let others just come to you.

- Create a play time—short bursts during the week and longer periods that you both can look forward to during the weekends.

- Put all her activities in your calendar—plan your weeks so you can be with her.

- Introduce her to your hobbies—create time to do it together.

- Put date night in the calendar—make it simple, or make it really special.

- Never knock off the to-do list alone—as you plan your running around, include her.

- Follow each other on social media—post together to capture moments.

- Listen more than you talk.

"we are God's workmanship, created in Christ Jesus which he prepared in advance to do good works."
Ephesians 2:10

CHAPTER FOUR
SELF-WORTH

I was reminded recently of how we allow others to put value on us. It was an extreme case of determining our self-worth that I will get to later in the chapter. Let me start with how we, as men, quite often determine it: We let spouses, friends, bosses or just about anyone determine our self-worth. We even allow inanimate objects to determine our value. We look at our position in our job, the salary we're being paid, the house we live in, the car we drive and, as we get older, the value of our retirement. All of these impact us; however, let's be real, we're men. We do let these impact us, but not in the way our girls do.

We have a way of just ignoring people's comments or getting angry enough about what is said that it drives us to do more. We're just wired differently. Your daughter is created in such a way that she is heavily impacted by those around her and what is said about her. She is extremely impacted by how the world in general defines girls. The world projects an image of what it means to be a young lady, and those around her will reinforce the definition. Us dads have to understand that our girls are affected so much more in this area of self-worth than we can even imagine. So pay attention.

Here is the extreme case that I alluded to earlier: An article recently came out about a young lady receiving a face transplant. The hook of the story pointed to her losing her face years prior, and now surgeons were placing a donated face on this young lady. I immediately wondered, *How did she lose her face?* Was it a run-in with a wild animal, was it a hunting accident or a fire that robbed her of her facial features? You had to read a long while before the reason for the loss of her face was shared. And much to my sadness, it revolved around this young lady's attempt to commit suicide. As I read further, the story unfolded in a similar fashion to stories I have read before. This precious young lady had experienced a few setbacks in her life that led to a sense of lacking value. Her family had moved a few times, which I'm sure led to friend struggles, as well as to a boy who wasn't loyal to their relationship. Each of these and probably other circumstances led to a question of, "Do I have value?" The world had convinced this young lady that friends, a boyfriend, etc., gave her value. The lies were so loud in her heart and head that she was convinced that the only way out was to end it all. I am sure she felt that no one cared. No one would miss her. Lies, Lies, Lies....

I know, this story is a little over the top, but I share this with a purpose. This is not the only time that I have heard about a young lady wanting to kill herself because of a lack of perceived value. It is way too common. And, this idea of self-worth is, next to her faith, the most important thing you must teach your daughter. She must know that she is created in God's image, which makes her extremely valuable. She is not a copy. God has not and will not make another angel like her. He has plans for her life and has placed her on earth with a purpose. Her identity is in Christ and Christ alone. You must guide her daily towards this idea. Guys, from a very young age, the world, through magazines, TV shows, movies, social media, music and even friends, will distort the view that God has intended for her. Let's be honest, the world is louder than you, but know God's power is louder and stronger. You must believe this and fight for her belief in the same.

Through your hang time, which you are now doing regularly, you get to assist your girl in the discovery of "who am I?" Knowing who she is will build her foundation. She is God's. On this journey, you have a front-row seat to all that she is. You can help her identify God's design of her, the one that makes her unique. God put our daughters on earth to accomplish special things that only they can do. No one else will fill the spot, not a teacher, a nurse and the list goes on.

Create an environment in which she can dream big. As she dreams, be the biggest cheerleader in her life. Spur her on with every dream regardless of how crazy or unrealistic you think it might be. Always keep in mind that God does have a plan, and His plans are always bigger than you or your daughter can imagine. So, let the dreams soar.

As you dream with your daughter, keep an eye out for what she is really good at. What seems to come effortlessly for her. It could be math, reading, kicking a ball, playing an instrument. The list is endless as to how God has gifted her. Shift your question a bit from her dreams and begin asking a new question, "What are you really good at?" Lead her on a path of discovery. As with the dreams, with your help she will identify what she's good at. The things she is really good at doing are gifts directly from God. Since God created it, don't get in the way, Dad. Support those gifts in any way you can. Give her time to practice her gifts. Create opportunities so she can flex that gift muscle as often as possible. With action and practice, the gift only gets stronger.

Now the fun really begins. The dreams are present. The gifts have been identified. And now you begin to see your daughter's passions. They come naturally because they match up with what God has given to her. She doesn't have to fight or fit in the world's box. She is just being her. How cool is that? We as dudes say that this is our sweet spot or that we're in the groove. You know the feeling. When the golf swing is perfect, you close the sale, the plan comes together. You are in the zone. It just happens. Heck, you can just talk about these things and your heart rate will literally go up. This is not by mistake when it happens to you, and the same promise is given to her. Remember He has a plan.

Can you see how this is unfolding? You are guiding your angel towards her worth and value in this world. God created her. You cultivate the dreams in her heart and head. That leads to you both discovering her God-given gifts and talents. Then boom. A passion arises in heart that God had from the very beginning. Dreams + gift/talents + passion = purpose = self-worth. No one can stand in the way of your girl's design. The world will try, but when she knows, I mean really knows her value because of God's plan/formula, the world will fall away. It works…Help her and fight for it.

You can and will guide her through the discovery of who she is and what she was created for; however, this will not be done in a vacuum. As much as you invest in hang time, the world around your angel will get more of her time, probably to a great degree, through social media. Social media has the ability to reach right into your girl's heart and head. Anytime, anyplace. The world's influence is in the palm of her hand. Marketers pump out who she should be and how she should look, which can truly impact her self-image. Never mind her watching others live a "perfect life" and stacking up herself against their lives. Oh what a destructive path this can take her down.

I hate to admit it; however, you are going to fight an uphill battle trying to remove this influence from her life. You can guide the path of exposure, though. Help her understand both the positive impact and destructive power that social media can have on her heart. Let her know that you are here to protect her, and encourage the positive ways this tool can be used.

I like to make it simple with my girls. When the world hits them, and they begin to devalue themselves, a few sets of emotions come over me. I encourage them to come over you as well. The emotion that typically comes naturally to us dudes is anger. Get angry at the world for the impact it is having. Pray that this influence would leave your daughter. Look at how you can remove its power by restricting situations, people, places that may have a negative impact. Be her safe harbor, where she can feel safety, love, comfort, when the world's waves hit. Let her share what is in her heart and how she feels. Listen, listen, listen. Be your daughter's biggest encourager. Remind her daily of her beauty, gifts and God's incredible creation. "God don't make no junk" is a Texas saying I use to remind my daughters of their incredible value. Simple but oh so true. Lift her up and send her out to impact the world with all the greatness that she is.

The YOUNG Girls

Abi, 22

A girl/woman's self-worth is easily the devil's favorite thing to attack. The devil has fed me lie after lie of how inadequate, unworthy and unattractive I am. At a young age, I would let these lies consume me and would lose sight of who I was in Christ. During these times, as I was growing up and learning how to fight the devil, my father was always there to guide me. He told me how adequate, worthy and beautiful I was (and am) because of whose I am. I am God's child. I was made perfect in HIS image. HE has given me countless gifts to use for the glory of His Kingdom. My father was a physical representation of the love and support our Heavenly Father gives.

When a young girl is continually being told how beautiful she is, how talented she is, and how she can achieve anything she sets her mind to, she will grow into a confident woman with tremendous goals. Because of my father, I have never felt that I was restricted by the world around me. I was always pushed to do more and do better for the cause of the gospel. The words you say and the time you give to build up your daughter's self-image will *truly* impact her for the rest of her life. It will help mold her into a strong woman of God!

Madi, 21

Self-worth is a hard one for girls. There are so many avenues, like church and friends and inspirational speakers, that continually try to empower girls to be the beautiful courageous girls we were made to be. But so often we are encouraged and empowered for that brief moment, then the world's reality hits us, be it through social media or a friend who is skinnier and more athletic or a family member who always seems a step ahead of you in the beauty department (the list goes on).

We have been told we are beautiful, irreplaceable, one of a kind, courageous and so much more, yet we so easily fail to believe it. Instead of listening to the people around us who truly love and care for us deeply, we try to find affirmation of our self-worth through social media or a silly boy at school. It's sad, but it's the reality so many girls live in today.

Firstly, what we really need is a rooted relationship with the Lord, our Father who made us for a purpose that no other girl on the face of the earth can fill. Secondly, we need a relationship with our dad that supports, encourages and equips that purpose. When there is a male figure in your life who genuinely loves and cares for you, it makes a *huge* difference in a girl's ability to fight those lies that the world tries to feed her. I encourage you dads to find your self-worth through the Lord, not through your spouse or your job or anything else, so that you can help your daughter do the same.

Emi, 19

The lack of feeling valued can make or break a girl's ability to live out her dreams and the path the Lord has for her. As a young girl, growing up as an athlete inside a "bougie" town, I thought the only way to do right was to be the best and go to school for a career that made a lot of money. This idea of value surrounded me and my thoughts for so long that it kept me from listening to the Lord and His plan for my life for more than seven years.

Think about it! Right now, in 2020, I am only nineteen. So for almost half of my life, my value was clouded by worldly views that I had on value.

Luckily, I have such a loving father who encouraged me to pray about my purpose and gain my value from only God. After much prayer and intentional conversations with my dad, I am now fully devoted to the will of the Lord for my life.

Lili, 18

As I was growing up, one thing that always affirmed my worth was my dad emphasizing that I was made in God's image. The biggest way to encourage your daughter to be grateful for who she is, is to point out how unique she is in different aspects of life. Emphasize that she does not have to be like everyone else even if it's the "popular" thing at the moment. Know that there is nothing you can do to keep her from seeing the world's image of who she is supposed to be, but you are one of the biggest influences in her life, so make her feel like she is priceless. I would rather my dad take action to do something that shows me that I am beautiful or loved rather than just saying it. That way I know that he put thought into it and really wants me to know it.

TAKE ACTION

- Ask your daughter what makes her feel both valued and devalued.

- Write on her mirror with a dry-erase marker words of value and encouragement.

- Post to social media special times together.

- Send texts at random.

- Create a journal where you write notes to her.

- Write a letter at Christmas for her stocking.

- On her birthday, have flowers and her favorite food ready for when she wakes up.

- Have regular date nights.

- Monitor and discuss her social media.

"All Scripture is breathed out by God and profitable for teaching, for reproof, for correction, and for training in righteousness," 2 Timothy 3:16

CHAPTER FIVE
DISCIPLINE – SETTING BOUNDARIES

When I was a senior in high school, I just had to go on a senior spring break trip. Nothing real fancy. A few friends headed to the Texas coast for a week of sun and fun. What I didn't realize, fancy or not, it costs money to go to the beach. Money which my parents were not willing to shovel out for my fun. So, what did I do? Go get a job at the local bowling alley. Now before you laugh, admit it, we all had jobs in high school that were not ideal; however, they paid the bills or, in my case, the job would pay for the big trip.

Surprisingly, I learned a lot at the bowling alley. I learned that striped referee shirts were cool (the uniform for a lane attendant), bowling is easy (though it takes some skill to do well) and kids need boundaries. Boundaries you ask? When a young kid came in to bowl, we would ask the child and parent, "Do you want kid rails for your game?" Without fail, the parent would say yes, and the child would emphatically say no. This was not the parents' first rodeo. They knew that kid rails would help little Susie have a better experience and score much higher. Now, little Susie didn't buy into this concept. She wanted to be a "big girl" and play without rails. Most of the time, the parent would give in to prove a point and keep Susie from causing a scene.

This scenario played out the same every time. After a few rolls down the lane, Susie would get frustrated and beg for the kiddie rails. She wanted to have more control over the overly heavy round object called a bowling ball and score better than her mom and dad. And wouldn't you know it, as soon as I put up the kid rails, both the parents and Susie had a much better experience, a fit was avoided, Susie rolled a good game and a little lesson on boundaries played out really well.

I surely did not realize that, so many years later, this experience would impact the raising of my daughters. Like the kids in a bowling alley, your daughter won't desire boundaries; however, in the game of life, boundaries are necessary. By nature, kids are a bit rebellious, so don't be surprised when she doesn't get excited when you draw up the rules. Even with a bit of rebellion, our girls want to be safe and avoid injury. Boundaries keep our girls from harm. Love protects them. Show her your love by setting boundaries.

Setting boundaries will include discipline when your angel just doesn't behave. Yes, this does and will happen at every age, so be prepared. Remember, whether she behaves well or not so well, it is a matter of her heart. Just like yours, her heart will choose to follow set boundaries or not. One key to shaping her heart is being aware of your emotions. For me anger could rear its ugly head because I was scared of what our daughters would experience as a result of their behavior. Whatever the reason, anger is always *bad*. Love for your daughter is the driver of discipline and should be experienced every time. Strive for it.

A second nugget to consider is the posture of discipline. You are naturally bigger and stronger than your girl at all stages. Unless your wife adds height to the gene pool, you will look down when speaking. Make sure you're on the same level when having a conversation. Kneel down or put her in your lap. Eye to eye is so important at every age. Your eyes should project your love and care for her. There will be times when you'll have to "grab" your daughter. Pull her away from a situation, pick her up or put your hands on her arm in the act of discipline. When this is the case, think of a hug. A hug can be strong and firm, but it doesn't hurt.

If you hold on to her heart too tightly, you'll crush it; hold on too softly, and you lose it. Strive for balance.

You cannot solve her behavior or actions with a heavy hand. Don't revert to how you solved problems in high school. A show of power, a loud voice, a raised fist or extreme emotion will ruin her. As a young dad, I didn't know any better. At least that was my excuse. I would get frustrated with a behavior and want to do what guys do. Solve it quickly, get loud and put some fear into my girls. Not a good idea at all. Every time I did this, my wife would repeat, "You are going to crush her heart."

Your end game is to draw her close, so you can teach her, not drive her away. This faulty tactic will drive her into a shell. Once she's in the shell, it is hard to draw her out. Over time, all she hears is noise and all she sees is anger. This will not work. I promise.

We don't want to crush our daughter's hearts; however, you can't retreat and sloppily hold her heart either. Sloppy usually means swinging to the side of "I'll just be her friend." Your daughter does not need another friend. She will have enough of those, both good and bad. You need to be the parent. Another dad tactic is to avoid the job of discipline altogether. They do the Heisman and leave it for Mom to take care of it. Don't be that guy. I've had my moments, of not stepping up and into the issue. Not a good idea. Without boundaries, she will take cues from others as to where the line is. Those cues come from the world, where everything is allowed. That formula will lead to pain and loss. As she gets older, these consequences will have a great impact on her heart.

For many years, I've been a part of an incredible ministry called Promise Makers and Girlz 4 God. The ministry focuses on the formation of Christ-like characteristics for sixth- through eighth-grade boys and girls. This prepares them for great choices as they enter high school and beyond. At the beginning of every school year, we teach a foundational "Traps" lesson to mimic the devil's schemes to trap our girls. We lay out different types of traps, from fly paper and mouse traps to small and, then, large animal traps. Each trap represents the escalation of the type of trap the devil sets and, more importantly, the consequences of the trap—consequences that can be avoided with the proper guide and boundaries set.

The girls get to see the traps and decide how to walk through them alone; however, before they begin the journey, we put a blindfold over their eyes. Clearly, at this point, they need a guide. In this case, the parent leads them through the traps. The guide tells them step by step how to walk, so the traps are not set off.

The guides use their voice or, at times, physical touch to set the boundaries so missteps don't happen. At times they have to stop their daughter and reset. Whatever it takes to avoid setting off a trap. Every time, once the exercise is complete, the one being led agrees that the help was needed.

In real life, as the parent, you see the traps (gossip, lying, stealing, drinking, etc.) and you might have even experienced some of these traps in your own life and know the consequences. You know that with each trap, the consequences increase. Some are temporary, but some are for life. Your loving discipline gives you the opportunity to *be* the consequences. Your consequences will be loving and caring towards your daughter. The world's natural discipline will not be.

I have been a city boy all of my life; however, one of our family's great adventures was being a part of starting a youth camp, Sabine Creek Ranch. We moved our four young girls into a very small barn apartment, literally among the stables of horses. I didn't know much about youth camp, living on a ranch or animals, including horses. Over the next few years, I was thrown into many unknown situations, including observing the training and raising of horses. We provided trail rides for our campers, so the horses had to be well trained and always on good behavior. We could not risk any injury, so it was quite a while before a horse was allowed to take folks on trail rides.

While we lived among the horses, I had a wonderful conversation comparing the training of horses to the raising of our daughters. The trainer told me to observe how training begins with a horse on a short lead in a small round pen. The first principle was for the horse to understand that, as long as it didn't listen to command, it would have very little room to move. Virtually no freedom. They could surely see their fellow horses out in pasture, with little restriction. They were free to roam.

As the horse began to comply with the training, two things happened. The lead was used less and less, and the round pen got bigger and bigger. Now, if the horse began to regress to bad behaviors, the lead was reattached and the pen got smaller. Freedom was reduced. As you can imagine, over time, the horse was released to the pasture and was able to take campers on trail rides.

Now that I have compared your daughter to a horse in training, let me explain. Our daughters want freedom, but it just can't be given all at once. It's to be gained as they show responsibility. As you create boundaries and they observe them, the amount of freedom increases. They are allowed to explore a bit more as they prove that they will obey what we have taught them. As with horses, as they make bad choices, you regain the control of making choices for them. It is so simple. Responsibility shown, more responsibility given.

My girls to this day refer to this as the "round pen" technique. I had a bit of an advantage because living on the ranch allowed them to see this at work firsthand. (You can jump ahead of me, skip the ranch life and show them a YouTube video.) In time, I could throw up the sign of a circle with my hands, and my girls knew that it could get larger or smaller based upon their behavior. The pen could be as large as hanging with friends on a Friday night or hanging with themselves in their room on a

Friday night. The cool part is that their choices determine their freedom. Their self-discipline determines their fate.

All the time that is spent "getting to know your daughter" really pays off when it comes to setting boundaries. A daughter that knows you will trust you in this area. A relationship built on trust builds great boundaries. She will know that your intentions are to protect her, point her towards who she wants to be and help her understand God's boundaries as well. Really, it is not about boundaries. It is not about discipline. It is about the changing of your daughter's heart.

A great way that we teach this in Team Promise Makers is with the acronym THRPPGEW (true, honorable, right, pure, pleasing, good, excellent, worthy of praise). A brilliant buddy of mine came up with this as a way to express Phil 4:8. "Finally brothers and sisters, whatever is true, whatever is honorable, whatever is just, whatever is pure, whatever is commendable, if there is any excellence, if there is anything worthy of praise, think about these things." These things lead to a pure heart. A pure heart makes good choices. Choices that your daughter will make if you do your job and set boundaries and discipline in love. You can do this, my brother!

The YOUNG Girls

Abi, 22

Man has my round pen been small in the past. I can distinctly remember, when Instagram was just becoming a thing, all my friends convinced me to make one despite my parents' rule that I could not have one. For weeks I had an account, and whenever my parents asked what I was doing on my phone, I would lie and tell them I was on Pinterest. Not a smart move…Though I was not doing anything bad on Instagram, I was just communicating with my inner circle of friends, I was deliberately disobeying *and* lying to my parents—a double whammy. It did not take long at all for my parents to figure out what I was doing, and the consequence was an immediate lack of responsibilities and trust.

It was hard for me to understand the "why" behind the "no social media" rule because at that age I did not realize what evil it could hold. There were a lot of boundaries that my parents set that I never understood; I just thought they were trying to restrict my fun. Despite the confusion, I tried my best to respect their wishes, which was not executed perfectly all the time. It was not until I moved away from home and started my independent life at Baylor that I realized how incredibly blessed I was with parents that cared enough to set boundaries. In college I became exposed to the world that my parents worked hard to protect me from while I was under their roof. It was the years that I spent in their protection that built me up to be able to turn away from the temptations Satan presents. Because of their loving guidance, discipline and explanation of why we follow Christ, I was able to walk the straight and narrow with more confidence. I finally understood "why" we as Christians say no to things the world finds attractive.

Be confident in the leadership of your daughter. It might take a long time for her to realize what you and her mother are trying to do, but *trust me*, if you stick to it, it pays off. You will be able to watch her make the right choices on her own when she is faced with grave hardships and decisions as an adult. You are responsible for showing her how Christians face temptation and stand confidently in Christ.

Madi, 21

Mutual trust between a father and daughter is key. Just like a true relationship with the Lord is built on faith, trusting even though we can't see or know, the same concept of trust works in a father–daughter relationship. If you don't trust her enough to let her fly, try new things in life or make "big girl" decisions, she will have a very hard time trusting you. She will start to rebel, because in her greatest attempts to earn your trust in her, she will continually fail. Failure is a good teacher in life, but too much of it can break a girl's heart or begin to build resentment in her heart. So try your hardest to, in a sense, let her go as she grows up and proves to you that you can trust her.

In my personal experience, having boundaries set is never fun or easy, but it has saved me from *so much* pain in life. I most times was reluctant to follow them at first, but over time I learned and experienced firsthand how they protected me and how they kept me on a better path. I am sitting here writing this at the age of twenty-one, and I know for a fact I would not be where I am today or who I am today if it wasn't for the boundaries I was raised on. They helped me ground my faith, establish self-worth, keep my purity (which is talked about in the next chapter), develop true life-long friendships and prevent unneeded pain that could have affected me for a lifetime. So just remember, she may not like them, but she will learn to be thankful for them. Take courage and be the father she needs you to be!

Emi, 19

I can promise you that as a young girl, I was not happy when "no" was the response. On the other hand, I would not be who I am today without the boundaries my dad set in my life. I wholeheartedly want to take these ideas and boundaries and apply them to my whole life and future family.

My favorite boundary, hard as it was to get over, was our movie/music restrictions. If you look back at the value chapter, one of the big factors in personal worth is worldly perception. While my sisters and I were growing up, we were only allowed to watch PG movies until we were fourteen, and even after that, we would check a movie's content before watching. We'd use a website called Plugged In to see what negative content was in the movie. For songs, my mom and dad would read the lyrics and check the message that was being portrayed. Because of this, I compared myself to others a lot less and grew up knowing foul language is not appropriate and is not of God's doing.

Lastly, when it comes to discipline, I will tell you, girls are just as stubborn as boys. We do not take physical punishment well because we will fight back, and for at least a few hours, look upon Dad negatively. I strongly agree with how my dad learned from his mistakes through God's truth. He allows God to guide him in the ways of discipline and setting boundaries.

Lili, 18

Throughout my growing up, I noticed how careful and caring my dad was when I had disobeyed. I noticed how sometimes, if he let his anger get the best of him, he would take a step back and come back in a calmer way.

I am very appreciative of all the things that my dad kept me from throughout the years. In the moment of him telling me I couldn't do something, I didn't understand and I would get upset, but looking back I realize how much heartbreak he kept me from. I know now that he was always protecting me and holding my heart oh so delicately, and he still is.

I truly believe that it is of the utmost importance to protect your daughter, but don't protect her so much that high school will be a slap in the face. No matter what you do, school will show her things that she has never seen. In those years, you can take the opportunity to show your daughter what is right and be with her along the way if she happens to stumble.

TAKE ACTION

- Remove negative emotion from your discipline.

- Always ask her "why" she is being disciplined to make sure you explained yourself clearly.

- Affirm her value in the midst of discipline.

- Finish with a hug and an "I love you."

- As she gets older, let her choose the boundaries and discipline.

- Discuss her heart's condition—behavior changes through the heart.

- Teach her to ask for forgiveness for inappropriate behavior.

- Celebrate a changed behavior/heart.

"Blessed are the pure in heart, for they shall see God."
Matthew 5:8

CHAPTER SIX
PURITY

A few years back, I was invited on an adventure of a lifetime. It was what we dudes call a "guys' trip" to end all trips. It was led by a friend who has the goal of climbing all the highest peaks in the world. His lofty goal should have been enough to tip us off that this would not be easy, right? But we didn't care. No, not this crew. We just focused on getting away from work and on fellowship with good friends. And maybe we were motivated just a little by "we climbed one of the highest peaks in the world" bragging rights, which never hurt a guy's ego.

Mount Whitney is a magnificent place with incredible views and more than enough challenges. Let's begin with the challenge of being at altitudes that a small pack of flatland dwellers should not consider. All the training in the world would not have prepared us for it. We might have gone slower due to our lack of exposure to high-altitude training, but it didn't stop us. As you can imagine, proper hydration, food and planned breaks became a big part of our trek up the mountain. We were required to break on schedule, and food was abundant in our backpacks; however, water was a challenge. We didn't "pack" a lot of water because it was heavy, and when climbing, heavy is never a part of the plan. So we had to find water along the way. Now you might think that's crazy, but high on a mountain with fresh runoff from snow, you are in good shape. We trusted our guides implicitly, so stream water it was. Each of us knelt down and filled our bottles to quench our thirst.

Can I just say, water from a mountain stream is the essence of pure. You can't see any cloudiness, dirt—nothing. No impurities. At least to the naked eye. And the taste. Oh man. Imagine the best glass of cold water you've ever paid money for, and you are not even close. This stuff was pure water!

Now, what does this have to do with your daughter? It has everything to do with her. Purity is a special thing. In the case of your daughter, much more special than a clear Nalgene water bottle filled on Mount Whitney. This is something you will fight hard to protect. The world will promote and quite forcefully lead her towards impurity. Just as we are tempted as men to impurity, so will your daughter be. The world will point her towards that dirty water in the creek. You must provide the guidance to point your daughter to pure water in a mountain stream.

Younger and younger, girls are pushed into relationships with what we in the Young household refer to as "dogs/boys." We aren't dogs anymore. Well, we shouldn't be. We are husbands and fathers. I hope and believe that you left your dog years behind you. But we can remember oh too well how we viewed and valued the need to be in a "relationship" with a young lady. We would do and say most anything to be around girls, and certainly to date one.

If the idea of "boys are dogs" isn't enough of a deterrent, the idea of saving dating for marriage is a great second line of defense against impurity. This might sound harsh or even cruel. *Brian, you're saying my girl has to be twenty-five or older before having a relationship with a boy?* Yes and no. Relationships with the opposite sex are essential to growing and maturing as a young lady. Having guys as friends is healthy and actually great for your daughter. She can learn how us guys function and affirm the "dog" belief. No, seriously. Having guy friends is essential.

This gets blurred when you cross over into dating, however. The move from friends to dating always carries a set of expectations. Expectations of exclusivity, of sharing one's deepest thoughts, of dreams and intimacy. With each step, your daughter's heart is exposed to new and exciting feelings towards a boy. Intimacy of the mind and heart in time will lead to physical intimacy. An intimacy created by God, but not for dating. The strongest of boundaries in a relationship can be set; however, the power of attraction and the world applauding this behavior will lead to impurity. Lead your daughter to understand that intimacy is a gift only in marriage.

Please know that "no dating unless for marriage" will come under scrutiny by your daughter. Of course it will, since this is not a norm for society. Be firm in your decision, though. The society that doesn't support you will be your best form of support: Unfortunately, young girls will date. Heck maybe your own daughter will "date" behind your back. Either way, wrecks and carnage will surely follow. How many times do we adhere to a rule once we see others get a ticket for breaking it (or we get a ticket ourselves) or, worse yet, get in a wreck? Every time. The sight of others crossing lines in relationships—of the heart damage it does—will be an affirmation of the "no dating unless for marriage policy." I promise you that your daughter will come to you with "you're right, Dad" after she sees a friend get injured in a relationship.

In our home, we celebrate this idea of purity. We mark this celebration with a special date and the presenting of a "purity ring." As best I can recall, the first time I was exposed to this idea was in the incredible movie *Courageous*. One of the dads takes his daughter on a special date to present her with a purity ring. This scene had a big impact on me and our girls.

Leading up to the age of thirteen, my daughter and I would begin planning our "True Love Waits" date. We call ours "True Love Waits" because it is the message on their rings from James Avery Jewelry. The idea was, she is entering the teen years and it's time to put a ring on it. Not to steal from the famous song by Beyoncé. But put a ring on it until the real ring of marriage is put on your daughter's finger. This ring is to remind her that she remains pure until the day that her wedding band is put on her finger by her husband. Until the day that she is at the altar, this ring will bind you and your daughter in promise: her promise to stay pure and yours to be there for her, to help with the hard and delicate relationship questions.

I recently walked by my first "True Love Waits" date restaurant, and the memories flooded back. Never mind my racing heart as I reflected on that night. I was scared to death. I have no problem speaking in front of large groups; however, this was bigger than that. I'll admit, I watched the scene in *Courageous* over and over again. I even had crib notes under my plate at the table so I didn't mess up. I came out the other side of that night patting myself on the back for not completely messing it up and so proud of my daughter for making this promise with me.

I'll conclude this chapter with a little humor and advice for you to share with your daughter. Of course, share as age appropriate.

To all the girls who are in a hurry to have a boyfriend or get married, a piece of Biblical advice: "Ruth patiently waited for her mate Boaz." While you are waiting on *your* Boaz, don't settle for any of his relatives: Broke-az, Po-az, Lying-az, Cheating-az, Dumb-az, Drunk-az, Cheap-az, Locked-up-az, Good-for-nothing-az, Lazy-az, and especially his third cousin Beating-yo-az...Wait on your Boaz, and make sure he respects Yoaz.

Okay if that was too harsh...I am sorry not sorry. I affirmed with many fellow dads and they confirmed this was necessary. So relax. Reread the text. Laugh and enjoy! You're welcome.

Purity is so very important, men. Everything that goes into your daughter leads to her heart. What she sees, hears and touches goes directly to her heart. You must protect her heart. The world wants it, and your job is to protect her against the world. Have conversations so you know her struggles. Listen and protect.

The YOUNG Girls

Abi, 22

I remember the night my dad and I had our "special" dinner the summer before I started middle school at the fine age of thirteen. I was full of emotions as I was getting ready. I felt like such a big girl and wanted everything to be perfect, but that excitement turned into stress within seconds as I was standing at the mirror absolutely hating what my hair looked like. Lol. So, as my dad was a nervous wreck downstairs, jotting down his script, I was busy worrying about how ugly my hair was—so typical. I can't help but laugh. Though the event started as a hot mess, we eventually got to the restaurant and had a wonderful time. Nearly 10 years later and I am just as, if not more, committed to that promise we made together.

Marriage is the most amazing covenant a man and woman can make together, as you know. As my heart was being guarded against boys in middle school, high school and early college, I was able to develop myself and focus my attention on pursuing Christ. I'd be lying if I said boys didn't distract my thoughts, but they haven't distracted me from my devotion to the Lord and my purity. Through my father's commitment to make purity an important topic, I have been saved from great potential heartbreak and temptation. Purity is a gift that can be taken away without your protection over her. Guard her and lead her through great seasons of singleness until, Lord willing, she has the chance at an amazing marriage to an incredible man that He has in store for her.

Madi, 21

Oh purity. I feel like anytime anyone reads/hears that word it immediately causes some kind of response, whether emotional or physical (anger, nervousness, full-body chill-bumps or tension). It's a touchy subject, and it has so many different messages circling around it. The world's saying, "Just do what you want," and the Lord's saying, "Wait, cherish your body (His temple) the way I created it to be cherished"—two completely different messages.

I have chosen to believe and follow the Lord's and to, day in and day out, fight the world's. It is *not* easy, and daughters will face so much hate, peer pressure, insecurity and more for following the Lord's message, but it is so worth it. It is another thing she will learn to be thankful for!

I am thankful for all the friendships I had with boys growing up because I learned, in a healthy way, about guys and how to love them as brothers in Christ. This helped me further establish myself as a woman, continually turning me to the Lord through it all, which has shown to be a huge blessing in my current relationship. I am the first Young girl to be in a relationship—twenty-one and in my first relationship…I know it's crazy if you look at it through the world's lenses. But I am so thankful that I waited on the Lord's plan/timing, which is *so* much better than mine! It has been an interesting change for my family, but it has been one of the coolest journeys. I cannot say enough how much of an impact my purity ring has had on my walk in faith and how I view relationships. It's a constant reminder on my left hand that the Lord has a bigger and better plan no matter what happens.

Emi, 19

Through saving dating for marriage, I have learned the importance of guarding my heart from unneeded stresses or "false love." The only love a young girl needs is from God and her father—not "false love" from an immature teenager that doesn't necessarily know what true love is.

I've taken away unnecessary drama and avoided many sinful temptations for the sake of waiting on God's bigger plan for my life. This does not mean that I haven't had guy friends that have strengthened my walk with the Lord or loved me as a sister in Christ. My dad has been the true example of a Christian man, yet through these friends, I have been able to experience the qualities that I will be looking for in a husband.

Lili, 18

If I'm being honest, purity revolves around one of a girl's biggest dreams: we want to marry our prince charming. Growing up, I took to heart how my dad cherished me and didn't let a boy make who I was. Because we as girls grow up with the image of trying to find the perfect boy, it can sometimes cause us to search among and experiment with different people, to see what qualities in a boy we like the most. But I challenged myself, and other girls to, instead, look to the men in the Bible to find the qualities I want in a guy. By doing this, us girls don't break our hearts with experimenting.

Let your daughter know that God will put the right man in her life when it is meant to be so to stay pure and guard her heart.

TAKE ACTION

- Make purity a topic of discussion early and often.

- Plan your "Purity Ceremony."

- Set boundaries of purity by limiting certain movies, books, TV, etc.

- Know her friends, especially the boys.

- Promote modesty—monitor what she wears.

- Listen and don't judge, to create an open dialogue about purity.

"Therefore, since we are surrounded by so great a cloud of witnesses, let us also lay aside every weight, and sin which clings so closely, and let us run with endurance the race that is set before us,"
Hebrews 12:1

CHAPTER SEVEN
ENDURANCE

I sat glued to my computer screen watching finisher after finisher run down the famous blue carpet at IronMan Arizona. A couple of my close buddies had dedicated more than a year of training to complete a race that most only dream about or completely dismiss, due to what it takes to not just finish but even *train* for.

I waited what seemed like hours to watch my buddy cross the finish line. In that moment, I was overwhelmed with emotion. Tears rolled down my face. As my wife walked in the room, she exclaimed, "Oh no, what's wrong?" I replied that we only go around the "Merry Go Round" of life one time and that "I have to do this!" "Do What?" she asked. "Do an IronMan!"

I was in my mid-thirties. Never swam, biked or ran much, and especially not to the distance of an IronMan. An IM, for those that don't know, much like I didn't know, is a 2.4-mile swim, 112-mile bike ride and 26.2-mile run. All three disciplines, back-to-back, on the same day. Oh yes, I thought just like you are right now, *NO WAY*. How in the world could I ever train my body to survive, much less finish, a race like that? One thing became abundantly clear: I was going to train a lot! But how and with whom?

One of the other guys that competed in the Arizona IronMan was one of my best friends to this day, Mason Randall. Mason is the kind of guy who has never backed down from a challenge or said no to anyone when they needed help. I asked Mason about his training and race experience. He shared that the training was extremely hard but that the race made every moment of pain worth it. I was so intrigued by our discussion that I was convinced I had to do the IM in Arizona the next year.

In order to make this happen, I needed someone to train me. I asked Mason if it was even possible to get ready for this type of distance in less than a year. He said it would be hard but that I should swim, bike and run every day along the way. He would train me. All he asked was that I listen to him and show up every day, ready to work. I accepted his very gracious offer, and so it began.

I met Mason every day for almost an entire year leading up to the big race. I honestly had no clue what I was doing. I would show up with my running shoes one day and then jump in the pool the next. Each day had its own set of challenges. About everyone told me I was crazy; however, those same people were amazed at what I was wanting to accomplish. I had my doubts, I wanted to quit, I had injuries, I felt pain, but most importantly, I wanted to finish an IronMan.

I went on to compete in my first IronMan, and three others followed as we grew the tribe of guys who had big dreams like me.

Those years of hard work and racing were some of the best of my life. I was able to work harder, endure more pain and accomplish more than I could have ever imagined. Every day required extreme dedication to the ultimate endurance sport.

I've looked at raising my girls much like training for and completing an IronMan. You only go around the "Merry Go Round" of life once, and you just have to do it. This must be the desire of your heart. The vision of your daughters thriving now and in the future has to be your fuel. Defeating the elements of the world must also be your fuel. When you focus on the prize, every step matters. You only get one chance to raise your girl. You have to take advantage of every day and every moment.

You will train daily so you can raise her day by day. Actually, *this* is the ultimate endurance sport. No joke. It appears to be such a daunting task: You've never done this before. You don't feel like you have the right equipment. The world will want you to do it much differently and at times tell you to quit. This is by no means a sprint. It is a long endurance race that will last a lifetime.

I've got you. More importantly, God's got you. I know that you are up for the task of being the fighter that your girl needs. You have dedicated time to read through the pages of this guide. That's a great start. Hopefully, you've begun doing the action items from each chapter. (You can go back to the chapters and actions year after year and even create your own.) You will make mistakes. Some days will be hard, and your will to win might take a hit. Please remember, you will rise up the next day and invest in your daughter once again. Grace is always available. Always! If you have messed up already or mess up in the future, grace is always there for you. It is never too late to start doing the right thing.

This is your moment! You have this. Beyond the pages of this book, know to always lean into God for guidance. That is the best way to achieve anything, including raising your girls. Be the warrior that your daughter needs—FIGHT FOR HER HEART! Become a Thriving Girl Dad!

Made in the USA
Las Vegas, NV
14 December 2021

37691411R00059